Keeping the

Family Fed

a Monthly Meal Planner

@ Journals and Notebooks

@ Journals & Notebooks

Copyright 2016

FOOD LOG

Date: / /

M T W T F S S

| BREAKFAST | NOTES | RATING |

SNACK

LUNCH

SNACK

DINNER

SNACK

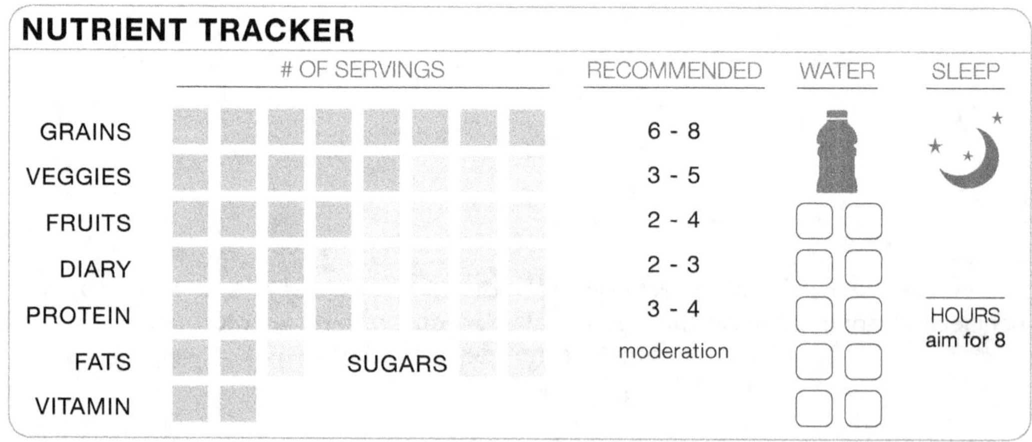

NUTRIENT TRACKER

	# OF SERVINGS	RECOMMENDED	WATER	SLEEP
GRAINS		6 - 8		
VEGGIES		3 - 5		
FRUITS		2 - 4		
DIARY		2 - 3		
PROTEIN		3 - 4		
FATS	SUGARS	moderation		HOURS aim for 8
VITAMIN				

FOOD LOG

Date: / /

M T W T F S S

| BREAKFAST | NOTES | RATING |

SNACK

LUNCH

SNACK

DINNER

SNACK

NUTRIENT TRACKER

	# OF SERVINGS	RECOMMENDED	WATER	SLEEP
GRAINS		6 - 8		
VEGGIES		3 - 5		
FRUITS		2 - 4		
DIARY		2 - 3		
PROTEIN		3 - 4		
FATS	SUGARS	moderation		HOURS
VITAMIN				aim for 8

FOOD LOG

Date: / /

M T W T F S S

| BREAKFAST | NOTES | RATING |

SNACK

LUNCH

SNACK

DINNER

SNACK

NUTRIENT TRACKER

	# OF SERVINGS	RECOMMENDED	WATER	SLEEP
GRAINS		6 - 8		
VEGGIES		3 - 5		
FRUITS		2 - 4		
DIARY		2 - 3		
PROTEIN		3 - 4		HOURS
FATS	SUGARS	moderation		aim for 8
VITAMIN				

FOOD LOG

Date: / /

M T W T F S S

BREAKFAST	NOTES	RATING
SNACK		
LUNCH		
SNACK		
DINNER		
SNACK		

NUTRIENT TRACKER

	# OF SERVINGS	RECOMMENDED	WATER	SLEEP
GRAINS		6 - 8		
VEGGIES		3 - 5		
FRUITS		2 - 4		
DIARY		2 - 3		
PROTEIN		3 - 4		
FATS	SUGARS	moderation		HOURS aim for 8
VITAMIN				

FOOD LOG

Date: / /

M T W T F S S

| BREAKFAST | NOTES | RATING |

SNACK

LUNCH

SNACK

DINNER

SNACK

NUTRIENT TRACKER

	# OF SERVINGS	RECOMMENDED	WATER	SLEEP
GRAINS		6 - 8		
VEGGIES		3 - 5		
FRUITS		2 - 4		
DIARY		2 - 3		
PROTEIN		3 - 4		
FATS	SUGARS	moderation		HOURS aim for 8
VITAMIN				

FOOD LOG

Date: ___ / ___ / ___

M T W T F S S

	BREAKFAST	NOTES	RATING
			🙂 😐 ☹️
	SNACK		🙂 😐 ☹️
	LUNCH		🙂 😐 ☹️
	SNACK		🙂 😐 ☹️
	DINNER		🙂 😐 ☹️
	SNACK		🙂 😐 ☹️

NUTRIENT TRACKER

	# OF SERVINGS	RECOMMENDED	WATER	SLEEP
GRAINS		6 - 8		
VEGGIES		3 - 5		
FRUITS		2 - 4		
DIARY		2 - 3		
PROTEIN		3 - 4		
FATS	SUGARS	moderation		HOURS aim for 8
VITAMIN				

FOOD LOG

Date: / /

M T W T F S S

BREAKFAST	NOTES	RATING
SNACK		
LUNCH		
SNACK		
DINNER		
SNACK		

NUTRIENT TRACKER

	# OF SERVINGS	RECOMMENDED	WATER	SLEEP
GRAINS		6 - 8		
VEGGIES		3 - 5		
FRUITS		2 - 4		
DIARY		2 - 3		
PROTEIN		3 - 4		
FATS	SUGARS	moderation		HOURS aim for 8
VITAMIN				

FOOD LOG

Date: / /

M T W T F S S

BREAKFAST	NOTES	RATING
SNACK		
LUNCH		
SNACK		
DINNER		
SNACK		

NUTRIENT TRACKER

	# OF SERVINGS	RECOMMENDED	WATER	SLEEP
GRAINS		6 - 8		
VEGGIES		3 - 5		
FRUITS		2 - 4		
DIARY		2 - 3		
PROTEIN		3 - 4		
FATS	SUGARS	moderation		HOURS aim for 8
VITAMIN				

FOOD LOG

Date: / /

M T W T F S S

| BREAKFAST | NOTES | RATING |

SNACK

LUNCH

SNACK

DINNER

SNACK

NUTRIENT TRACKER

	# OF SERVINGS	RECOMMENDED	WATER	SLEEP
GRAINS		6 - 8		
VEGGIES		3 - 5		
FRUITS		2 - 4		
DIARY		2 - 3		
PROTEIN		3 - 4		
FATS	SUGARS	moderation		HOURS aim for 8
VITAMIN				

FOOD LOG

Date: / /   M T W T F S S

	BREAKFAST	NOTES	RATING

BREAKFAST — NOTES — RATING

SNACK — NOTES — RATING

LUNCH — NOTES — RATING

SNACK — NOTES — RATING

DINNER — NOTES — RATING

SNACK — NOTES — RATING

NUTRIENT TRACKER

	# OF SERVINGS	RECOMMENDED	WATER	SLEEP
GRAINS		6 - 8		
VEGGIES		3 - 5		
FRUITS		2 - 4		
DIARY		2 - 3		
PROTEIN		3 - 4		
FATS	SUGARS	moderation		HOURS aim for 8
VITAMIN				

FOOD LOG

Date: / /   ☐☐☐☐☐☐☐
M T W T F S S

| BREAKFAST | NOTES | RATING |

| SNACK | NOTES | RATING |

| LUNCH | NOTES | RATING |

| SNACK | NOTES | RATING |

| DINNER | NOTES | RATING |

| SNACK | NOTES | RATING |

NUTRIENT TRACKER

	# OF SERVINGS	RECOMMENDED	WATER	SLEEP
GRAINS		6 - 8		
VEGGIES		3 - 5		
FRUITS		2 - 4		
DIARY		2 - 3		
PROTEIN		3 - 4		
FATS	SUGARS	moderation		HOURS aim for 8
VITAMIN				

FOOD LOG

Date: / /

M T W T F S S

BREAKFAST	NOTES	RATING
		🙂 😐 🙁
SNACK	NOTES	🙂 😐 🙁
LUNCH	NOTES	🙂 😐 🙁
SNACK	NOTES	🙂 😐 🙁
DINNER	NOTES	🙂 😐 🙁
SNACK	NOTES	🙂 😐 🙁

NUTRIENT TRACKER

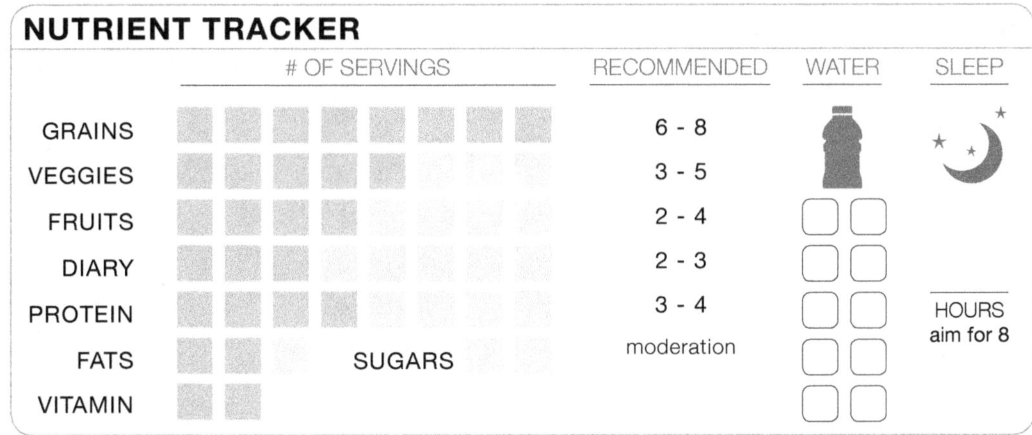

	# OF SERVINGS	RECOMMENDED	WATER	SLEEP
GRAINS		6 - 8		
VEGGIES		3 - 5		
FRUITS		2 - 4		
DIARY		2 - 3		
PROTEIN		3 - 4		
FATS	SUGARS	moderation		HOURS aim for 8
VITAMIN				

FOOD LOG

Date: / /   M T W T F S S

| BREAKFAST | NOTES | RATING |

SNACK

LUNCH

SNACK

DINNER

SNACK

NUTRIENT TRACKER

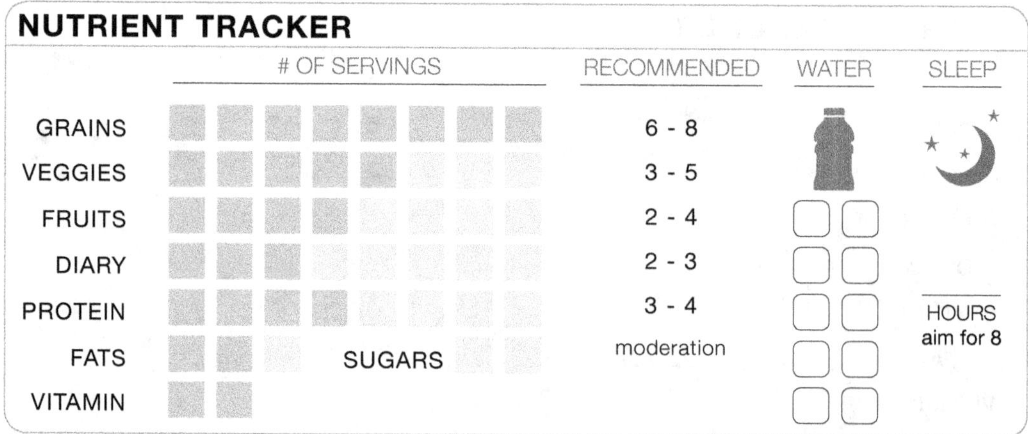

	# OF SERVINGS	RECOMMENDED	WATER	SLEEP
GRAINS		6 - 8		
VEGGIES		3 - 5		
FRUITS		2 - 4		
DIARY		2 - 3		
PROTEIN		3 - 4		
FATS	SUGARS	moderation		HOURS aim for 8
VITAMIN				

FOOD LOG

Date: /   /   M T W T F S S

BREAKFAST	NOTES	RATING
SNACK		
LUNCH		
SNACK		
DINNER		
SNACK		

NUTRIENT TRACKER

	# OF SERVINGS	RECOMMENDED	WATER	SLEEP
GRAINS		6 - 8		
VEGGIES		3 - 5		
FRUITS		2 - 4		
DIARY		2 - 3		
PROTEIN		3 - 4		
FATS	SUGARS	moderation		
VITAMIN				HOURS aim for 8

FOOD LOG

Date: /   /

M T W T F S S

| BREAKFAST | NOTES | RATING |

SNACK

LUNCH

SNACK

DINNER

SNACK

NUTRIENT TRACKER

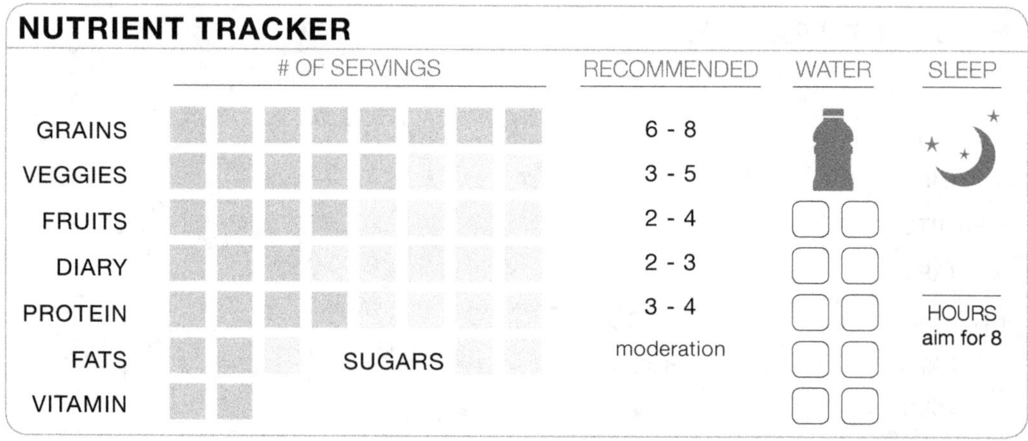

	# OF SERVINGS	RECOMMENDED	WATER	SLEEP
GRAINS		6 - 8		
VEGGIES		3 - 5		
FRUITS		2 - 4		
DIARY		2 - 3		
PROTEIN		3 - 4		
FATS	SUGARS	moderation		HOURS aim for 8
VITAMIN				

FOOD LOG

Date: ___ / ___ / ___

M T W T F S S

BREAKFAST	NOTES	RATING
		😊 😐 ☹
SNACK		😊 😐 ☹
LUNCH		😊 😐 ☹
SNACK		😊 😐 ☹
DINNER		😊 😐 ☹
SNACK		😊 😐 ☹

NUTRIENT TRACKER

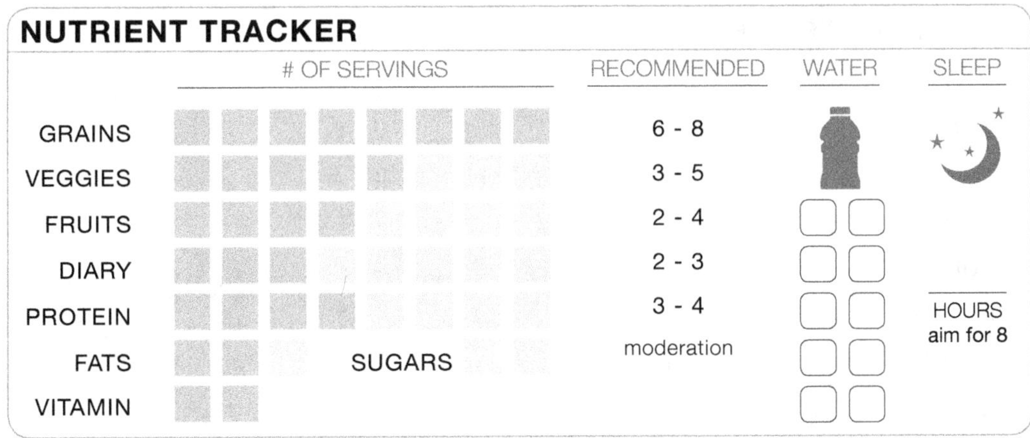

	# OF SERVINGS	RECOMMENDED	WATER	SLEEP
GRAINS		6 - 8		
VEGGIES		3 - 5		
FRUITS		2 - 4		
DIARY		2 - 3		
PROTEIN		3 - 4		
FATS	SUGARS	moderation		HOURS aim for 8
VITAMIN				

FOOD LOG

Date: / /

M T W T F S S

| BREAKFAST | NOTES | RATING |

SNACK

LUNCH

SNACK

DINNER

SNACK

NUTRIENT TRACKER

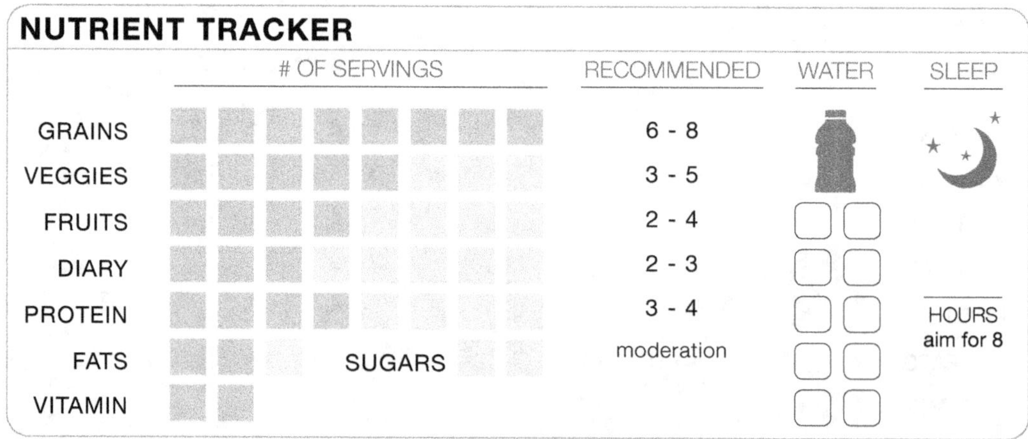

	# OF SERVINGS	RECOMMENDED	WATER	SLEEP
GRAINS		6 - 8		
VEGGIES		3 - 5		
FRUITS		2 - 4		
DIARY		2 - 3		
PROTEIN		3 - 4		
FATS	SUGARS	moderation		HOURS aim for 8
VITAMIN				

FOOD LOG

Date: / /

M T W T F S S

BREAKFAST	NOTES	RATING
		🙂 😐 🙁
SNACK		🙂 😐 🙁
LUNCH		🙂 😐 🙁
SNACK		🙂 😐 🙁
DINNER		🙂 😐 🙁
SNACK		🙂 😐 🙁

NUTRIENT TRACKER

	# OF SERVINGS	RECOMMENDED	WATER	SLEEP
GRAINS		6 - 8		
VEGGIES		3 - 5		
FRUITS		2 - 4		
DIARY		2 - 3		
PROTEIN		3 - 4		
FATS	SUGARS	moderation		HOURS aim for 8
VITAMIN				

FOOD LOG

Date: / /

M T W T F S S

BREAKFAST	NOTES	RATING
SNACK	NOTES	RATING
LUNCH	NOTES	RATING
SNACK	NOTES	RATING
DINNER	NOTES	RATING
SNACK	NOTES	RATING

NUTRIENT TRACKER

	# OF SERVINGS	RECOMMENDED	WATER	SLEEP
GRAINS		6 - 8		
VEGGIES		3 - 5		
FRUITS		2 - 4		
DIARY		2 - 3		
PROTEIN		3 - 4		
FATS	SUGARS	moderation		HOURS aim for 8
VITAMIN				

FOOD LOG

Date: /   /

M T W T F S S

	BREAKFAST	NOTES	RATING
BREAKFAST			:) :| :(
SNACK			:) :| :(
LUNCH			:) :| :(
SNACK			:) :| :(
DINNER			:) :| :(
SNACK			:) :| :(

NUTRIENT TRACKER

	# OF SERVINGS	RECOMMENDED	WATER	SLEEP
GRAINS		6 - 8		
VEGGIES		3 - 5		
FRUITS		2 - 4		
DIARY		2 - 3		
PROTEIN		3 - 4		
FATS	SUGARS	moderation		HOURS aim for 8
VITAMIN				

FOOD LOG

Date: / /

M T W T F S S

	BREAKFAST	NOTES	RATING
	SNACK		
	LUNCH		
	SNACK		
	DINNER		
	SNACK		

NUTRIENT TRACKER

	# OF SERVINGS	RECOMMENDED	WATER	SLEEP
GRAINS		6 - 8		
VEGGIES		3 - 5		
FRUITS		2 - 4		
DIARY		2 - 3		
PROTEIN		3 - 4		
FATS	SUGARS	moderation		HOURS aim for 8
VITAMIN				

FOOD LOG

Date: /   /

M T W T F S S

BREAKFAST	NOTES	RATING

SNACK

LUNCH

SNACK

DINNER

SNACK

NUTRIENT TRACKER

	# OF SERVINGS	RECOMMENDED	WATER	SLEEP
GRAINS		6 - 8		
VEGGIES		3 - 5		
FRUITS		2 - 4		
DIARY		2 - 3		
PROTEIN		3 - 4		
FATS	SUGARS	moderation		
VITAMIN				

HOURS
aim for 8

FOOD LOG

Date: / /

M T W T F S S

| BREAKFAST | NOTES | RATING |

SNACK

LUNCH

SNACK

DINNER

SNACK

NUTRIENT TRACKER

	# OF SERVINGS	RECOMMENDED	WATER	SLEEP
GRAINS		6 - 8		
VEGGIES		3 - 5		
FRUITS		2 - 4		
DIARY		2 - 3		
PROTEIN		3 - 4		
FATS	SUGARS	moderation		HOURS aim for 8
VITAMIN				

FOOD LOG

Date: / /

M T W T F S S

| BREAKFAST | NOTES | RATING |

SNACK

LUNCH

SNACK

DINNER

SNACK

NUTRIENT TRACKER

	# OF SERVINGS	RECOMMENDED	WATER	SLEEP
GRAINS		6 - 8		
VEGGIES		3 - 5		
FRUITS		2 - 4		
DIARY		2 - 3		
PROTEIN		3 - 4		
FATS	SUGARS	moderation		HOURS aim for 8
VITAMIN				

FOOD LOG

Date: / /

M T W T F S S

BREAKFAST	NOTES	RATING

SNACK

LUNCH

SNACK

DINNER

SNACK

NUTRIENT TRACKER

	# OF SERVINGS	RECOMMENDED	WATER	SLEEP
GRAINS		6 - 8		
VEGGIES		3 - 5		
FRUITS		2 - 4		
DIARY		2 - 3		
PROTEIN		3 - 4		
FATS	SUGARS	moderation		HOURS aim for 8
VITAMIN				

FOOD LOG

Date: / /

M T W T F S S

BREAKFAST	NOTES	RATING
SNACK		
LUNCH		
SNACK		
DINNER		
SNACK		

NUTRIENT TRACKER

	# OF SERVINGS	RECOMMENDED	WATER	SLEEP
GRAINS		6 - 8		
VEGGIES		3 - 5		
FRUITS		2 - 4		
DIARY		2 - 3		
PROTEIN		3 - 4		
FATS	SUGARS	moderation		HOURS aim for 8
VITAMIN				

FOOD LOG

Date: / /

M T W T F S S

| BREAKFAST | NOTES | RATING |

SNACK

LUNCH

SNACK

DINNER

SNACK

NUTRIENT TRACKER

	# OF SERVINGS	RECOMMENDED	WATER	SLEEP
GRAINS		6 - 8		
VEGGIES		3 - 5		
FRUITS		2 - 4		
DIARY		2 - 3		
PROTEIN		3 - 4		
FATS	SUGARS	moderation		
VITAMIN				

HOURS
aim for 8

FOOD LOG

Date: / /

M T W T F S S

BREAKFAST	NOTES	RATING
SNACK		
LUNCH		
SNACK		
DINNER		
SNACK		

NUTRIENT TRACKER

	# OF SERVINGS	RECOMMENDED	WATER	SLEEP
GRAINS		6 - 8		
VEGGIES		3 - 5		
FRUITS		2 - 4		
DIARY		2 - 3		
PROTEIN		3 - 4		
FATS	SUGARS	moderation		
VITAMIN				

HOURS
aim for 8

FOOD LOG

Date: / /

M T W T F S S

BREAKFAST	NOTES	RATING
SNACK	NOTES	RATING
LUNCH	NOTES	RATING
SNACK	NOTES	RATING
DINNER	NOTES	RATING
SNACK	NOTES	RATING

NUTRIENT TRACKER

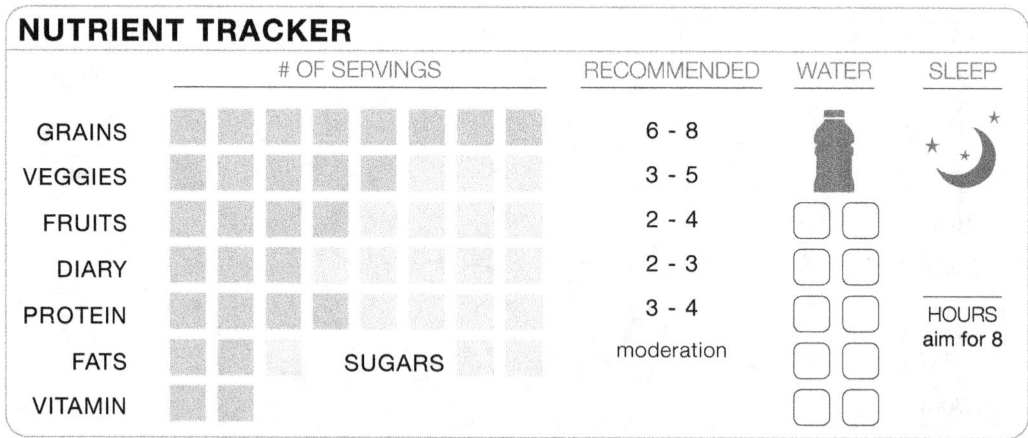

	# OF SERVINGS	RECOMMENDED	WATER	SLEEP
GRAINS		6 - 8		
VEGGIES		3 - 5		
FRUITS		2 - 4		
DIARY		2 - 3		
PROTEIN		3 - 4		
FATS	SUGARS	moderation		HOURS aim for 8
VITAMIN				

FOOD LOG

Date: / /

M T W T F S S

BREAKFAST	NOTES	RATING
SNACK		
LUNCH		
SNACK		
DINNER		
SNACK		

NUTRIENT TRACKER

	# OF SERVINGS	RECOMMENDED	WATER	SLEEP
GRAINS		6 - 8		
VEGGIES		3 - 5		
FRUITS		2 - 4		
DIARY		2 - 3		
PROTEIN		3 - 4		
FATS	SUGARS	moderation		
VITAMIN				

HOURS
aim for 8

FOOD LOG

Date: / /

M T W T F S S

BREAKFAST	NOTES	RATING

SNACK

LUNCH

SNACK

DINNER

SNACK

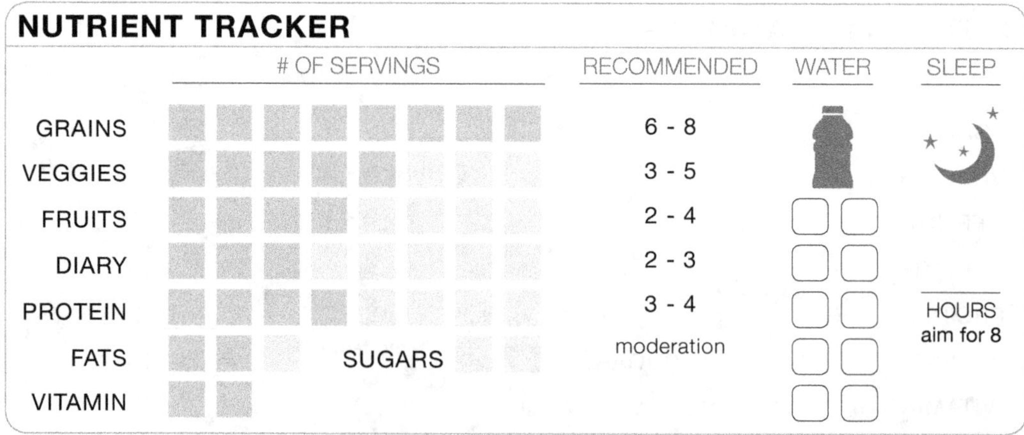

NUTRIENT TRACKER

	# OF SERVINGS	RECOMMENDED	WATER	SLEEP
GRAINS		6 - 8		
VEGGIES		3 - 5		
FRUITS		2 - 4		
DIARY		2 - 3		
PROTEIN		3 - 4		
FATS	SUGARS	moderation		HOURS aim for 8
VITAMIN				

FOOD LOG

Date: / /

M T W T F S S

BREAKFAST	NOTES	RATING
SNACK		
LUNCH		
SNACK		
DINNER		
SNACK		

NUTRIENT TRACKER

	# OF SERVINGS	RECOMMENDED	WATER	SLEEP
GRAINS		6 - 8		
VEGGIES		3 - 5		
FRUITS		2 - 4		
DIARY		2 - 3		
PROTEIN		3 - 4		
FATS	SUGARS	moderation		HOURS aim for 8
VITAMIN				

FOOD LOG

Date: /   /

M T W T F S S

| BREAKFAST | NOTES | RATING |

SNACK

LUNCH

SNACK

DINNER

SNACK

NUTRIENT TRACKER

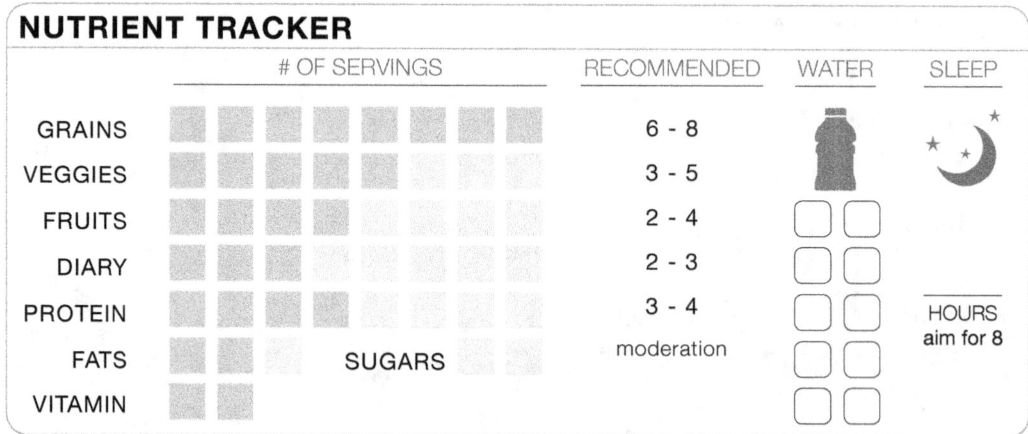

FOOD LOG

Date: / /

M T W T F S S

| BREAKFAST | NOTES | RATING |

SNACK

LUNCH

SNACK

DINNER

SNACK

NUTRIENT TRACKER

	# OF SERVINGS	RECOMMENDED	WATER	SLEEP
GRAINS		6 - 8		
VEGGIES		3 - 5		
FRUITS		2 - 4		
DIARY		2 - 3		
PROTEIN		3 - 4		
FATS	SUGARS	moderation		HOURS aim for 8
VITAMIN				

FOOD LOG

Date: / /

M T W T F S S

| BREAKFAST | NOTES | RATING |

SNACK

LUNCH

SNACK

DINNER

SNACK

NUTRIENT TRACKER

	# OF SERVINGS	RECOMMENDED	WATER	SLEEP
GRAINS		6 - 8		
VEGGIES		3 - 5		
FRUITS		2 - 4		
DIARY		2 - 3		
PROTEIN		3 - 4		
FATS	SUGARS	moderation		HOURS aim for 8
VITAMIN				

FOOD LOG

Date: /   /

M T W T F S S

| BREAKFAST | NOTES | RATING |

SNACK

LUNCH

SNACK

DINNER

SNACK

NUTRIENT TRACKER

	# OF SERVINGS	RECOMMENDED	WATER	SLEEP
GRAINS		6 - 8		
VEGGIES		3 - 5		
FRUITS		2 - 4		
DIARY		2 - 3		
PROTEIN		3 - 4		
FATS	SUGARS	moderation		HOURS aim for 8
VITAMIN				

FOOD LOG

Date: / / | M T W T F S S |

| BREAKFAST | NOTES | RATING |

☺ ☻ ☹

SNACK

☺ ☻ ☹

LUNCH

☺ ☻ ☹

SNACK

☺ ☻ ☹

DINNER

☺ ☻ ☹

SNACK

☺ ☻ ☹

NUTRIENT TRACKER

	# OF SERVINGS	RECOMMENDED	WATER	SLEEP
GRAINS		6 - 8		
VEGGIES		3 - 5		
FRUITS		2 - 4		
DIARY		2 - 3		
PROTEIN		3 - 4		
FATS	SUGARS	moderation		HOURS aim for 8
VITAMIN				

FOOD LOG

Date: / /

M T W T F S S

BREAKFAST	NOTES	RATING

SNACK

LUNCH

SNACK

DINNER

SNACK

NUTRIENT TRACKER

	# OF SERVINGS	RECOMMENDED	WATER	SLEEP
GRAINS		6 - 8		
VEGGIES		3 - 5		
FRUITS		2 - 4		
DIARY		2 - 3		
PROTEIN		3 - 4		
FATS	SUGARS	moderation		HOURS aim for 8
VITAMIN				

FOOD LOG

Date: /   /

M T W T F S S

BREAKFAST	NOTES	RATING
		:) :| :(
SNACK		:) :| :(
LUNCH		:) :| :(
SNACK		:) :| :(
DINNER		:) :| :(
SNACK		:) :| :(

NUTRIENT TRACKER

	# OF SERVINGS	RECOMMENDED	WATER	SLEEP
GRAINS		6 - 8		
VEGGIES		3 - 5		
FRUITS		2 - 4		
DIARY		2 - 3		
PROTEIN		3 - 4		
FATS	SUGARS	moderation		HOURS aim for 8
VITAMIN				

FOOD LOG

Date: _ / _ / _

M T W T F S S

BREAKFAST	NOTES	RATING
SNACK		
LUNCH		
SNACK		
DINNER		
SNACK		

NUTRIENT TRACKER

	# OF SERVINGS	RECOMMENDED	WATER	SLEEP
GRAINS		6 - 8		
VEGGIES		3 - 5		
FRUITS		2 - 4		
DIARY		2 - 3		
PROTEIN		3 - 4		
FATS	SUGARS	moderation		HOURS aim for 8
VITAMIN				

FOOD LOG

Date: / /

M T W T F S S

| BREAKFAST | NOTES | RATING |

SNACK

LUNCH

SNACK

DINNER

SNACK

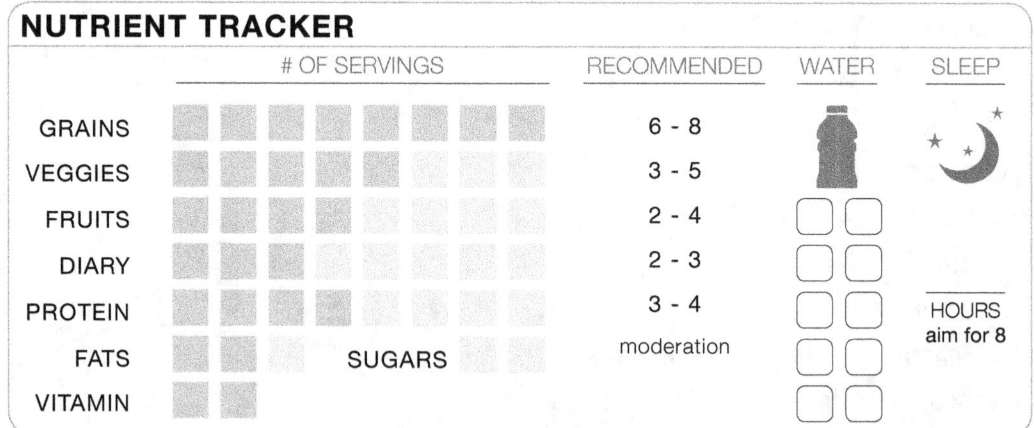

NUTRIENT TRACKER

	# OF SERVINGS	RECOMMENDED	WATER	SLEEP
GRAINS		6 - 8		
VEGGIES		3 - 5		
FRUITS		2 - 4		
DIARY		2 - 3		
PROTEIN		3 - 4		
FATS	SUGARS	moderation		HOURS aim for 8
VITAMIN				

FOOD LOG

Date: / /

M T W T F S S

| BREAKFAST | NOTES | RATING |

SNACK

LUNCH

SNACK

DINNER

SNACK

NUTRIENT TRACKER

	# OF SERVINGS	RECOMMENDED	WATER	SLEEP
GRAINS		6 - 8		
VEGGIES		3 - 5		
FRUITS		2 - 4		
DIARY		2 - 3		
PROTEIN		3 - 4		
FATS	SUGARS	moderation		HOURS aim for 8
VITAMIN				

FOOD LOG

Date: / /

M T W T F S S

| BREAKFAST | NOTES | RATING |

SNACK

LUNCH

SNACK

DINNER

SNACK

NUTRIENT TRACKER

	# OF SERVINGS	RECOMMENDED	WATER	SLEEP
GRAINS		6 - 8		
VEGGIES		3 - 5		
FRUITS		2 - 4		
DIARY		2 - 3		
PROTEIN		3 - 4		
FATS	SUGARS	moderation		HOURS aim for 8
VITAMIN				

FOOD LOG

Date: / /

M T W T F S S

BREAKFAST	NOTES	RATING

SNACK

LUNCH

SNACK

DINNER

SNACK

NUTRIENT TRACKER

	# OF SERVINGS	RECOMMENDED	WATER	SLEEP
GRAINS		6 - 8		
VEGGIES		3 - 5		
FRUITS		2 - 4		
DIARY		2 - 3		
PROTEIN		3 - 4		HOURS
FATS	SUGARS	moderation		aim for 8
VITAMIN				

FOOD LOG
Date: /   /
M T W T F S S
BREAKFAST
NOTES
RATING
SNACK
LUNCH
SNACK
DINNER
SNACK

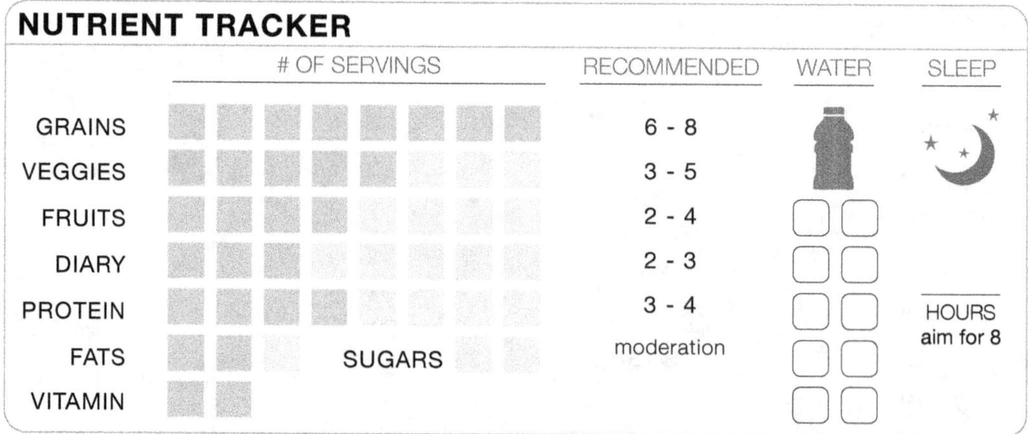

NUTRIENT TRACKER
OF SERVINGS
RECOMMENDED
WATER
SLEEP
GRAINS
6 - 8
VEGGIES
3 - 5
FRUITS
2 - 4
DIARY
2 - 3
PROTEIN
3 - 4
FATS
SUGARS
moderation
VITAMIN
HOURS
aim for 8

FOOD LOG

Date: / /

M T W T F S S

| BREAKFAST | NOTES | RATING |

SNACK

LUNCH

SNACK

DINNER

SNACK

NUTRIENT TRACKER

	# OF SERVINGS	RECOMMENDED	WATER	SLEEP
GRAINS		6 - 8		
VEGGIES		3 - 5		
FRUITS		2 - 4		
DIARY		2 - 3		
PROTEIN		3 - 4		
FATS	SUGARS	moderation		HOURS aim for 8
VITAMIN				

FOOD LOG

Date: / /

M T W T F S S

| BREAKFAST | NOTES | RATING |

| SNACK | | |

| LUNCH | | |

| SNACK | | |

| DINNER | | |

| SNACK | | |

NUTRIENT TRACKER

	# OF SERVINGS	RECOMMENDED	WATER	SLEEP
GRAINS		6 - 8		
VEGGIES		3 - 5		
FRUITS		2 - 4		
DIARY		2 - 3		
PROTEIN		3 - 4		
FATS	SUGARS	moderation		HOURS aim for 8
VITAMIN				

FOOD LOG

Date: / /

M T W T F S S

| BREAKFAST | NOTES | RATING |

SNACK

LUNCH

SNACK

DINNER

SNACK

NUTRIENT TRACKER

	# OF SERVINGS	RECOMMENDED	WATER	SLEEP
GRAINS		6 - 8		
VEGGIES		3 - 5		
FRUITS		2 - 4		
DIARY		2 - 3		
PROTEIN		3 - 4		
FATS	SUGARS	moderation		HOURS aim for 8
VITAMIN				

FOOD LOG

Date: / /

M T W T F S S

BREAKFAST	NOTES	RATING
SNACK		
LUNCH		
SNACK		
DINNER		
SNACK		

NUTRIENT TRACKER

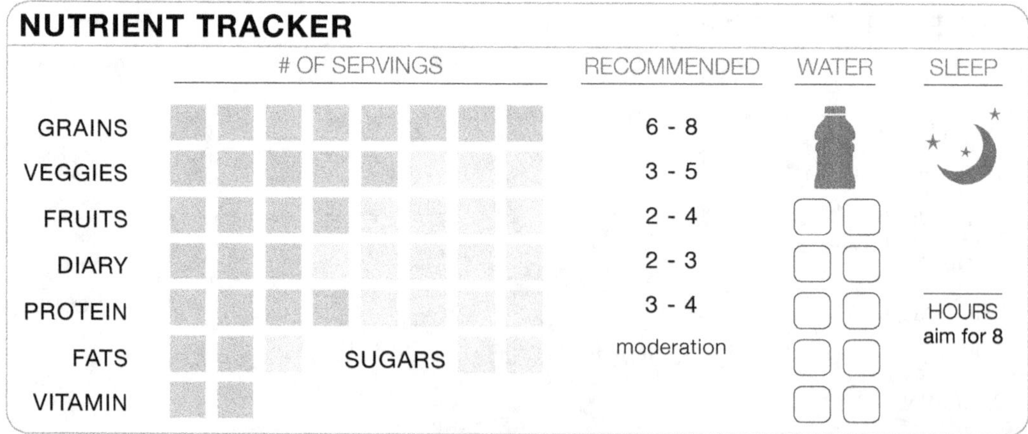

	# OF SERVINGS	RECOMMENDED	WATER	SLEEP
GRAINS		6 - 8		
VEGGIES		3 - 5		
FRUITS		2 - 4		
DIARY		2 - 3		
PROTEIN		3 - 4		
FATS	SUGARS	moderation		HOURS aim for 8
VITAMIN				

FOOD LOG

Date: ___ / ___ / ___

M T W T F S S

BREAKFAST	NOTES	RATING
		😊 😐 ☹️

SNACK	NOTES	RATING
		😊 😐 ☹️

LUNCH	NOTES	RATING
		😊 😐 ☹️

SNACK	NOTES	RATING
		😊 😐 ☹️

DINNER	NOTES	RATING
		😊 😐 ☹️

SNACK	NOTES	RATING
		😊 😐 ☹️

NUTRIENT TRACKER

	# OF SERVINGS	RECOMMENDED	WATER	SLEEP
GRAINS		6 - 8		
VEGGIES		3 - 5		
FRUITS		2 - 4		
DIARY		2 - 3		
PROTEIN		3 - 4		
FATS	SUGARS	moderation		
VITAMIN				

HOURS
aim for 8

FOOD LOG

Date: / /   M T W T F S S

BREAKFAST	NOTES	RATING
		☺ 😐 ☹
SNACK		☺ 😐 ☹
LUNCH		☺ 😐 ☹
SNACK		☺ 😐 ☹
DINNER		☺ 😐 ☹
SNACK		☺ 😐 ☹

NUTRIENT TRACKER

	# OF SERVINGS	RECOMMENDED	WATER	SLEEP
GRAINS		6 - 8		
VEGGIES		3 - 5		
FRUITS		2 - 4		
DIARY		2 - 3		
PROTEIN		3 - 4		
FATS	SUGARS	moderation		HOURS aim for 8
VITAMIN				

FOOD LOG

Date: /   /

M T W T F S S

BREAKFAST	NOTES	RATING
SNACK		
LUNCH		
SNACK		
DINNER		
SNACK		

NUTRIENT TRACKER

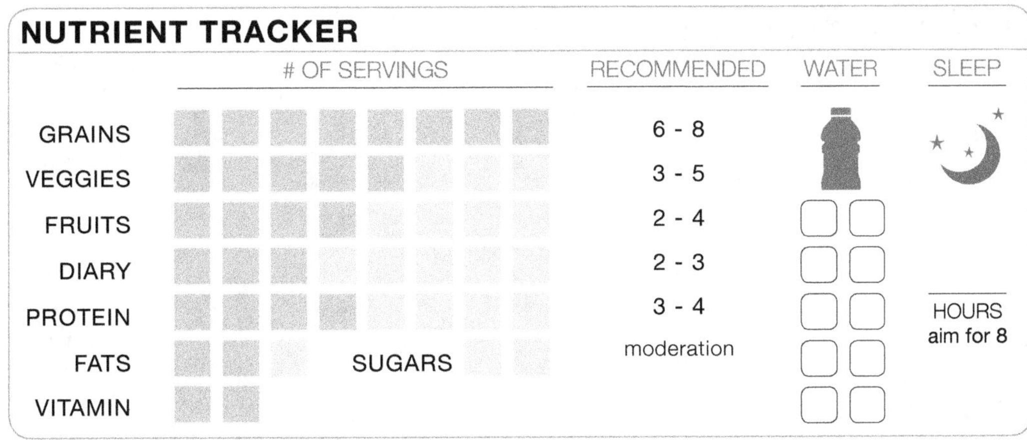

	# OF SERVINGS	RECOMMENDED	WATER	SLEEP
GRAINS		6 - 8		
VEGGIES		3 - 5		
FRUITS		2 - 4		
DIARY		2 - 3		
PROTEIN		3 - 4		HOURS aim for 8
FATS	SUGARS	moderation		
VITAMIN				

FOOD LOG

Date: /   /

M T W T F S S

BREAKFAST	NOTES	RATING

| SNACK | | |

| LUNCH | | |

| SNACK | | |

| DINNER | | |

| SNACK | | |

NUTRIENT TRACKER

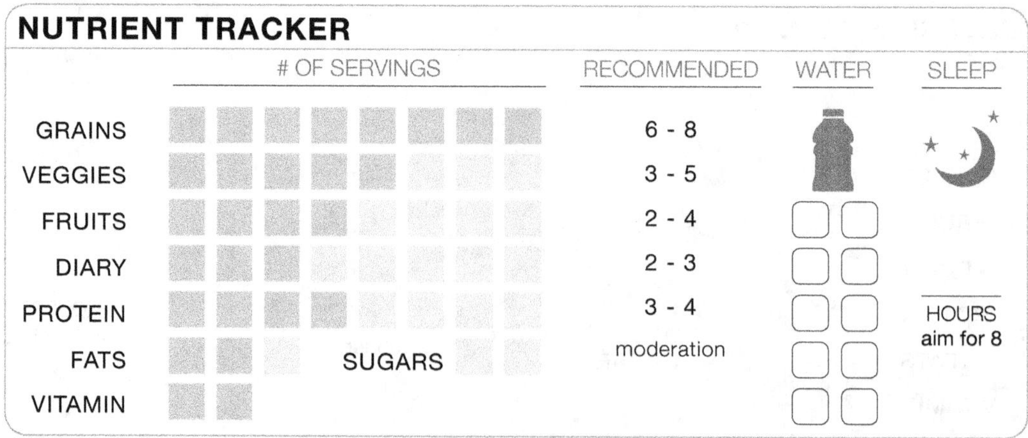

	# OF SERVINGS	RECOMMENDED	WATER	SLEEP
GRAINS		6 - 8		
VEGGIES		3 - 5		
FRUITS		2 - 4		
DIARY		2 - 3		
PROTEIN		3 - 4		
FATS	SUGARS	moderation		HOURS aim for 8
VITAMIN				

FOOD LOG

Date: / /

M T W T F S S

| BREAKFAST | NOTES | RATING |

SNACK

LUNCH

SNACK

DINNER

SNACK

NUTRIENT TRACKER

	# OF SERVINGS	RECOMMENDED	WATER	SLEEP
GRAINS		6 - 8		
VEGGIES		3 - 5		
FRUITS		2 - 4		
DIARY		2 - 3		
PROTEIN		3 - 4		
FATS	SUGARS	moderation		HOURS aim for 8
VITAMIN				

FOOD LOG

Date: /   /

M T W T F S S

BREAKFAST	NOTES	RATING

SNACK

LUNCH

SNACK

DINNER

SNACK

NUTRIENT TRACKER

	# OF SERVINGS	RECOMMENDED	WATER	SLEEP
GRAINS		6 - 8		
VEGGIES		3 - 5		
FRUITS		2 - 4		
DIARY		2 - 3		
PROTEIN		3 - 4		
FATS	SUGARS	moderation		HOURS aim for 8
VITAMIN				

FOOD LOG

Date: / /

M T W T F S S

BREAKFAST	NOTES	RATING

SNACK

LUNCH

SNACK

DINNER

SNACK

NUTRIENT TRACKER

	# OF SERVINGS	RECOMMENDED	WATER	SLEEP
GRAINS		6 - 8		
VEGGIES		3 - 5		
FRUITS		2 - 4		
DIARY		2 - 3		
PROTEIN		3 - 4		HOURS aim for 8
FATS	SUGARS	moderation		
VITAMIN				

FOOD LOG

Date: / /

M T W T F S S

| BREAKFAST | NOTES | RATING |

SNACK

LUNCH

SNACK

DINNER

SNACK

NUTRIENT TRACKER

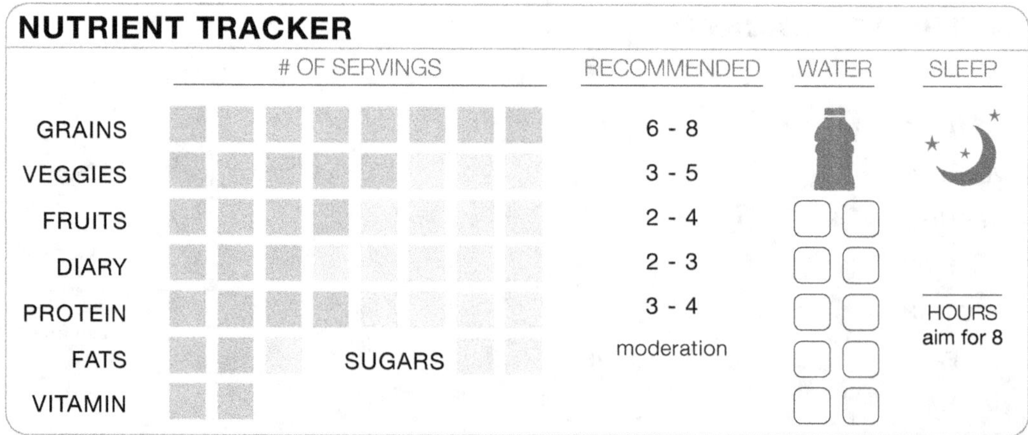

	# OF SERVINGS	RECOMMENDED	WATER	SLEEP
GRAINS		6 - 8		
VEGGIES		3 - 5		
FRUITS		2 - 4		
DIARY		2 - 3		
PROTEIN		3 - 4		
FATS	SUGARS	moderation		HOURS aim for 8
VITAMIN				

FOOD LOG

Date: / /

M T W T F S S

| BREAKFAST | NOTES | RATING |

BREAKFAST

SNACK

LUNCH

SNACK

DINNER

SNACK

NUTRIENT TRACKER

	# OF SERVINGS	RECOMMENDED	WATER	SLEEP
GRAINS		6 - 8		
VEGGIES		3 - 5		
FRUITS		2 - 4		
DIARY		2 - 3		
PROTEIN		3 - 4		
FATS	SUGARS	moderation		
VITAMIN				HOURS aim for 8

FOOD LOG

Date: / /

M T W T F S S

| BREAKFAST | NOTES | RATING |

SNACK

LUNCH

SNACK

DINNER

SNACK

NUTRIENT TRACKER

	# OF SERVINGS	RECOMMENDED	WATER	SLEEP
GRAINS		6 - 8		
VEGGIES		3 - 5		
FRUITS		2 - 4		
DIARY		2 - 3		
PROTEIN		3 - 4		
FATS	SUGARS	moderation		HOURS aim for 8
VITAMIN				

FOOD LOG

Date: / /

M T W T F S S

| BREAKFAST | NOTES | RATING |

SNACK

LUNCH

SNACK

DINNER

SNACK

NUTRIENT TRACKER

	# OF SERVINGS	RECOMMENDED	WATER	SLEEP
GRAINS		6 - 8		
VEGGIES		3 - 5		
FRUITS		2 - 4		
DIARY		2 - 3		
PROTEIN		3 - 4		
FATS	SUGARS	moderation		HOURS aim for 8
VITAMIN				

FOOD LOG

Date: / /

M T W T F S S

BREAKFAST	NOTES	RATING

| SNACK | | |

| LUNCH | | |

| SNACK | | |

| DINNER | | |

| SNACK | | |

NUTRIENT TRACKER

	# OF SERVINGS	RECOMMENDED	WATER	SLEEP
GRAINS		6 - 8		
VEGGIES		3 - 5		
FRUITS		2 - 4		
DIARY		2 - 3		
PROTEIN		3 - 4		
FATS	SUGARS	moderation		HOURS aim for 8
VITAMIN				

FOOD LOG

Date: / /

M T W T F S S

| BREAKFAST | NOTES | RATING |

| SNACK | | |

| LUNCH | | |

| SNACK | | |

| DINNER | | |

| SNACK | | |

NUTRIENT TRACKER

	# OF SERVINGS	RECOMMENDED	WATER	SLEEP
GRAINS		6 - 8		
VEGGIES		3 - 5		
FRUITS		2 - 4		
DIARY		2 - 3		
PROTEIN		3 - 4		
FATS	SUGARS	moderation		
VITAMIN				

HOURS
aim for 8

FOOD LOG

Date: / /

M T W T F S S

| BREAKFAST | NOTES | RATING |

SNACK

LUNCH

SNACK

DINNER

SNACK

NUTRIENT TRACKER

	# OF SERVINGS	RECOMMENDED	WATER	SLEEP
GRAINS		6 - 8		
VEGGIES		3 - 5		
FRUITS		2 - 4		
DIARY		2 - 3		
PROTEIN		3 - 4		
FATS	SUGARS	moderation		HOURS aim for 8
VITAMIN				

FOOD LOG

Date: ___ / ___ / ___

M T W T F S S

BREAKFAST	NOTES	RATING
SNACK		
LUNCH		
SNACK		
DINNER		
SNACK		

NUTRIENT TRACKER

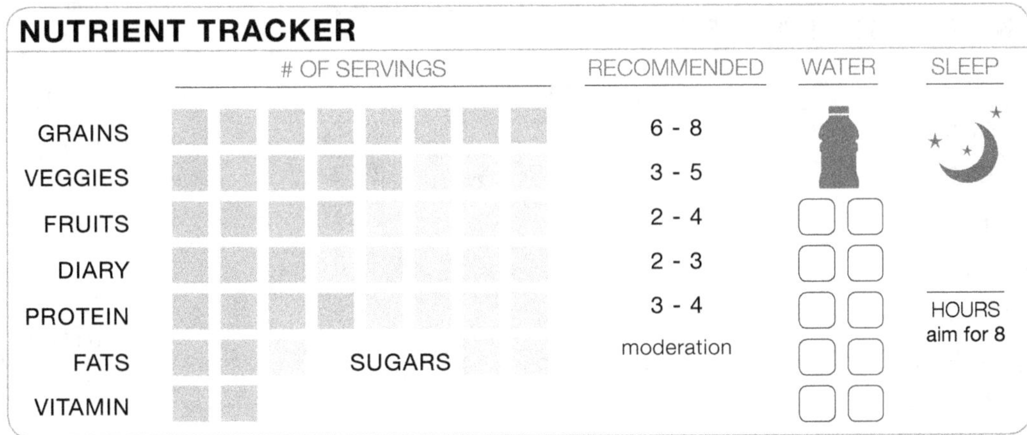

	# OF SERVINGS	RECOMMENDED	WATER	SLEEP
GRAINS		6 - 8		
VEGGIES		3 - 5		
FRUITS		2 - 4		
DIARY		2 - 3		
PROTEIN		3 - 4		
FATS	SUGARS	moderation		HOURS aim for 8
VITAMIN				

FOOD LOG

Date: /   /

M T W T F S S

BREAKFAST	NOTES	RATING
		🙂 😐 ☹
SNACK		🙂 😐 ☹
LUNCH		🙂 😐 ☹
SNACK		🙂 😐 ☹
DINNER		🙂 😐 ☹
SNACK		🙂 😐 ☹

NUTRIENT TRACKER

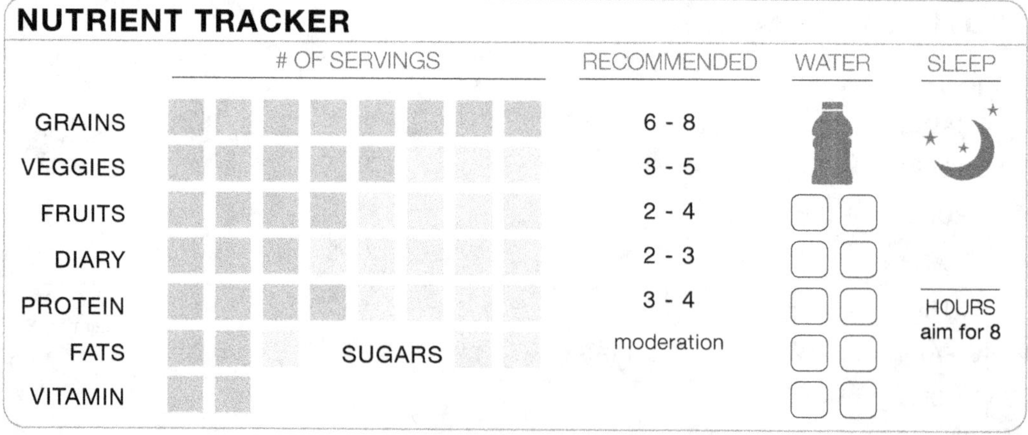

	# OF SERVINGS	RECOMMENDED	WATER	SLEEP
GRAINS		6 - 8		
VEGGIES		3 - 5		
FRUITS		2 - 4		
DIARY		2 - 3		
PROTEIN		3 - 4		
FATS	SUGARS	moderation		HOURS aim for 8
VITAMIN				

FOOD LOG

Date: / /   M T W T F S S

BREAKFAST	NOTES	RATING
		:) :| :(

SNACK		RATING
		:) :| :(

LUNCH		RATING
		:) :| :(

SNACK		RATING
		:) :| :(

DINNER		RATING
		:) :| :(

SNACK		RATING
		:) :| :(

NUTRIENT TRACKER

	# OF SERVINGS	RECOMMENDED	WATER	SLEEP
GRAINS		6 - 8		
VEGGIES		3 - 5		
FRUITS		2 - 4		
DIARY		2 - 3		
PROTEIN		3 - 4		HOURS aim for 8
FATS	SUGARS	moderation		
VITAMIN				

FOOD LOG

Date: / /

M T W T F S S

| BREAKFAST | NOTES | RATING |

SNACK

LUNCH

SNACK

DINNER

SNACK

NUTRIENT TRACKER

	# OF SERVINGS	RECOMMENDED	WATER	SLEEP
GRAINS		6 - 8		
VEGGIES		3 - 5		
FRUITS		2 - 4		
DIARY		2 - 3		
PROTEIN		3 - 4		
FATS	SUGARS	moderation		HOURS aim for 8
VITAMIN				

FOOD LOG

Date: / /

M T W T F S S

| BREAKFAST | NOTES | RATING |

SNACK

LUNCH

SNACK

DINNER

SNACK

NUTRIENT TRACKER

	# OF SERVINGS	RECOMMENDED	WATER	SLEEP
GRAINS		6 - 8		
VEGGIES		3 - 5		
FRUITS		2 - 4		
DIARY		2 - 3		
PROTEIN		3 - 4		
FATS	SUGARS	moderation		HOURS aim for 8
VITAMIN				

FOOD LOG

Date: / /

M T W T F S S

BREAKFAST	NOTES	RATING
		:) :| :(
SNACK		:) :| :(
LUNCH		:) :| :(
SNACK		:) :| :(
DINNER		:) :| :(
SNACK		:) :| :(

NUTRIENT TRACKER

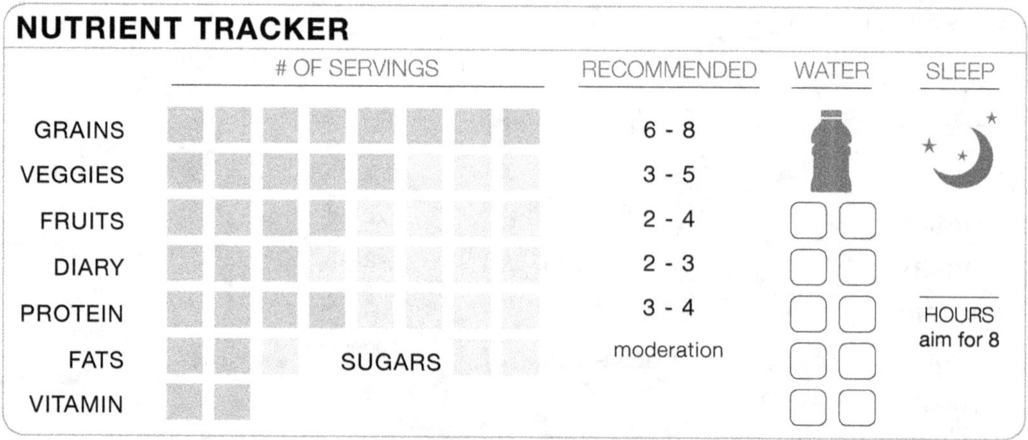

	# OF SERVINGS	RECOMMENDED	WATER	SLEEP
GRAINS		6 - 8		
VEGGIES		3 - 5		
FRUITS		2 - 4		
DIARY		2 - 3		
PROTEIN		3 - 4		
FATS	SUGARS	moderation		HOURS aim for 8
VITAMIN				

FOOD LOG

Date: /   /

M T W T F S S

BREAKFAST	NOTES	RATING

BREAKFAST

NOTES

RATING

SNACK

LUNCH

SNACK

DINNER

SNACK

NUTRIENT TRACKER

	# OF SERVINGS	RECOMMENDED	WATER	SLEEP
GRAINS		6 - 8		
VEGGIES		3 - 5		
FRUITS		2 - 4		
DIARY		2 - 3		
PROTEIN		3 - 4		
FATS	SUGARS	moderation		HOURS aim for 8
VITAMIN				

FOOD LOG

Date: / /

M T W T F S S

| BREAKFAST | NOTES | RATING |

☺ ☺ ☹

SNACK

☺ ☺ ☹

LUNCH

☺ ☺ ☹

SNACK

☺ ☺ ☹

DINNER

☺ ☺ ☹

SNACK

☺ ☺ ☹

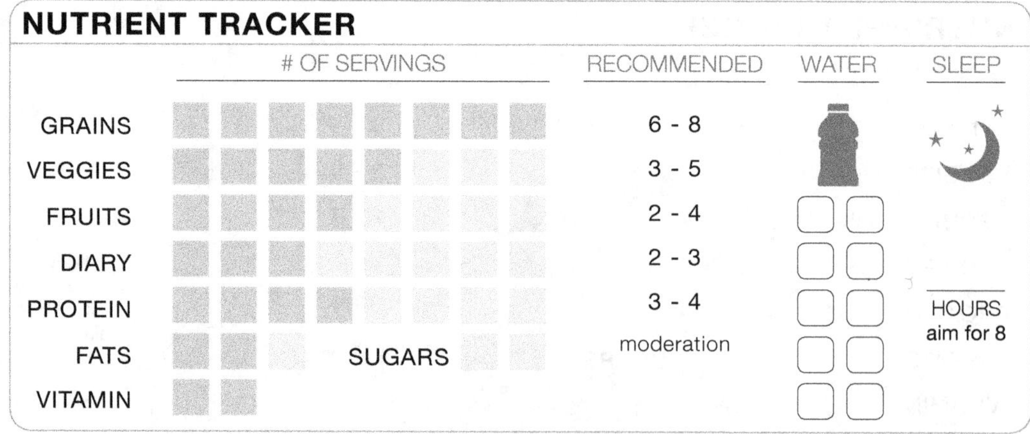

NUTRIENT TRACKER

	# OF SERVINGS	RECOMMENDED	WATER	SLEEP
GRAINS		6 - 8		
VEGGIES		3 - 5		
FRUITS		2 - 4		
DIARY		2 - 3		
PROTEIN		3 - 4		
FATS	SUGARS	moderation		HOURS aim for 8
VITAMIN				

FOOD LOG

Date: / /

M T W T F S S

| BREAKFAST | NOTES | RATING |

SNACK

LUNCH

SNACK

DINNER

SNACK

NUTRIENT TRACKER

	# OF SERVINGS	RECOMMENDED	WATER	SLEEP
GRAINS		6 - 8		
VEGGIES		3 - 5		
FRUITS		2 - 4		
DIARY		2 - 3		
PROTEIN		3 - 4		
FATS	SUGARS	moderation		
VITAMIN				

HOURS
aim for 8

FOOD LOG

Date: / /

M T W T F S S

| BREAKFAST | NOTES | RATING |

SNACK

LUNCH

SNACK

DINNER

SNACK

NUTRIENT TRACKER

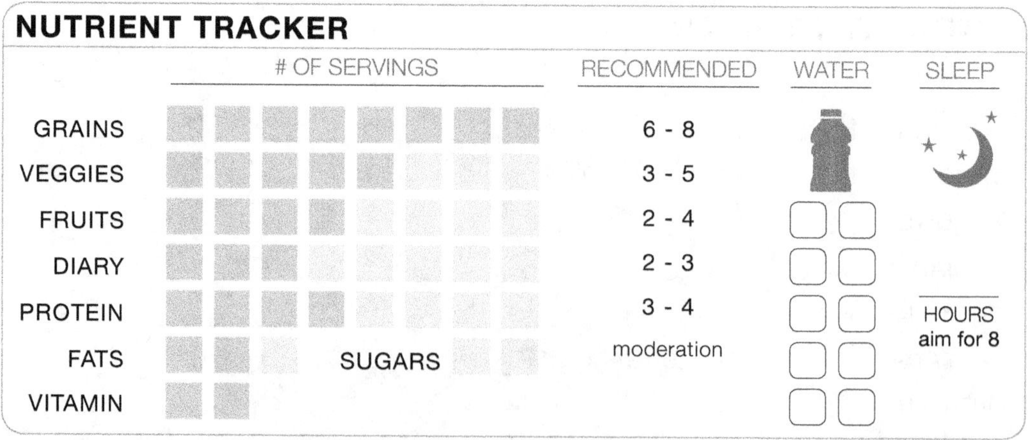

	# OF SERVINGS	RECOMMENDED	WATER	SLEEP
GRAINS		6 - 8		
VEGGIES		3 - 5		
FRUITS		2 - 4		
DIARY		2 - 3		
PROTEIN		3 - 4		
FATS	SUGARS	moderation		HOURS aim for 8
VITAMIN				

FOOD LOG

Date: / /

M T W T F S S

BREAKFAST	NOTES	RATING

SNACK

LUNCH

SNACK

DINNER

SNACK

NUTRIENT TRACKER

	# OF SERVINGS	RECOMMENDED	WATER	SLEEP
GRAINS		6 - 8		
VEGGIES		3 - 5		
FRUITS		2 - 4		
DIARY		2 - 3		
PROTEIN		3 - 4		
FATS	SUGARS	moderation		HOURS aim for 8
VITAMIN				

FOOD LOG

Date: / /

M T W T F S S

| BREAKFAST | NOTES | RATING |

SNACK

LUNCH

SNACK

DINNER

SNACK

NUTRIENT TRACKER

	# OF SERVINGS	RECOMMENDED	WATER	SLEEP
GRAINS		6 - 8		
VEGGIES		3 - 5		
FRUITS		2 - 4		
DIARY		2 - 3		
PROTEIN		3 - 4		
FATS	SUGARS	moderation		
VITAMIN				HOURS aim for 8

FOOD LOG

Date: / /

M T W T F S S

BREAKFAST	NOTES	RATING

SNACK

LUNCH

SNACK

DINNER

SNACK

NUTRIENT TRACKER

	# OF SERVINGS	RECOMMENDED	WATER	SLEEP
GRAINS		6 - 8		
VEGGIES		3 - 5		
FRUITS		2 - 4		
DIARY		2 - 3		
PROTEIN		3 - 4		
FATS	SUGARS	moderation		
VITAMIN				

HOURS
aim for 8

FOOD LOG

Date: / /

M T W T F S S

| BREAKFAST | NOTES | RATING |

SNACK

LUNCH

SNACK

DINNER

SNACK

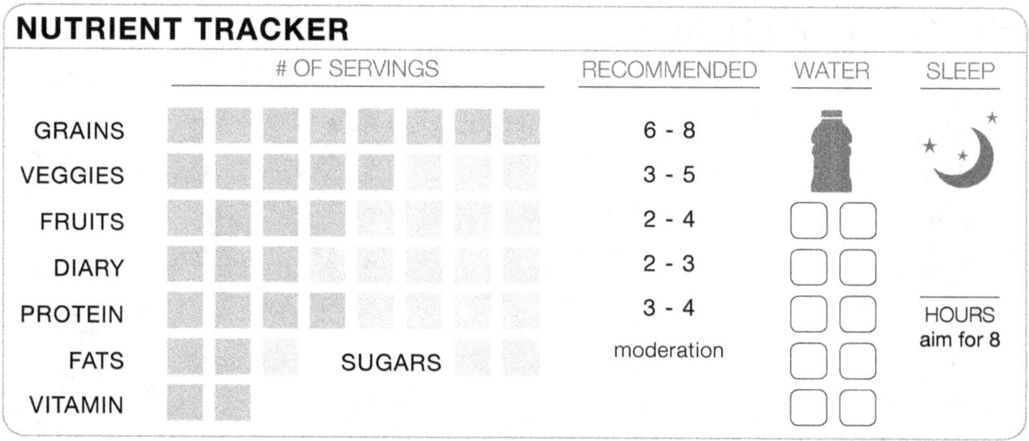

NUTRIENT TRACKER

	# OF SERVINGS	RECOMMENDED	WATER	SLEEP
GRAINS		6 - 8		
VEGGIES		3 - 5		
FRUITS		2 - 4		
DIARY		2 - 3		
PROTEIN		3 - 4		HOURS aim for 8
FATS	SUGARS	moderation		
VITAMIN				

FOOD LOG

Date: / /

M T W T F S S

BREAKFAST	NOTES	RATING
SNACK		
LUNCH		
SNACK		
DINNER		
SNACK		

NUTRIENT TRACKER

	# OF SERVINGS	RECOMMENDED	WATER	SLEEP
GRAINS		6 - 8		
VEGGIES		3 - 5		
FRUITS		2 - 4		
DIARY		2 - 3		
PROTEIN		3 - 4		
FATS	SUGARS	moderation		HOURS aim for 8
VITAMIN				

FOOD LOG

Date: / /

M T W T F S S

BREAKFAST	NOTES	RATING
SNACK		
LUNCH		
SNACK		
DINNER		
SNACK		

NUTRIENT TRACKER

	# OF SERVINGS	RECOMMENDED	WATER	SLEEP
GRAINS		6 - 8		
VEGGIES		3 - 5		
FRUITS		2 - 4		
DIARY		2 - 3		
PROTEIN		3 - 4		
FATS	SUGARS	moderation		HOURS aim for 8
VITAMIN				

FOOD LOG

Date: / /

M T W T F S S

| BREAKFAST | NOTES | RATING |

| SNACK | NOTES | RATING |

| LUNCH | NOTES | RATING |

| SNACK | NOTES | RATING |

| DINNER | NOTES | RATING |

| SNACK | NOTES | RATING |

NUTRIENT TRACKER

	# OF SERVINGS	RECOMMENDED	WATER	SLEEP
GRAINS		6 - 8		
VEGGIES		3 - 5		
FRUITS		2 - 4		
DIARY		2 - 3		
PROTEIN		3 - 4		
FATS	SUGARS	moderation		HOURS aim for 8
VITAMIN				

FOOD LOG

Date: /   /

M T W T F S S

BREAKFAST	NOTES	RATING
		🙂 😐 ☹️
SNACK		🙂 😐 ☹️
LUNCH		🙂 😐 ☹️
SNACK		🙂 😐 ☹️
DINNER		🙂 😐 ☹️
SNACK		🙂 😐 ☹️

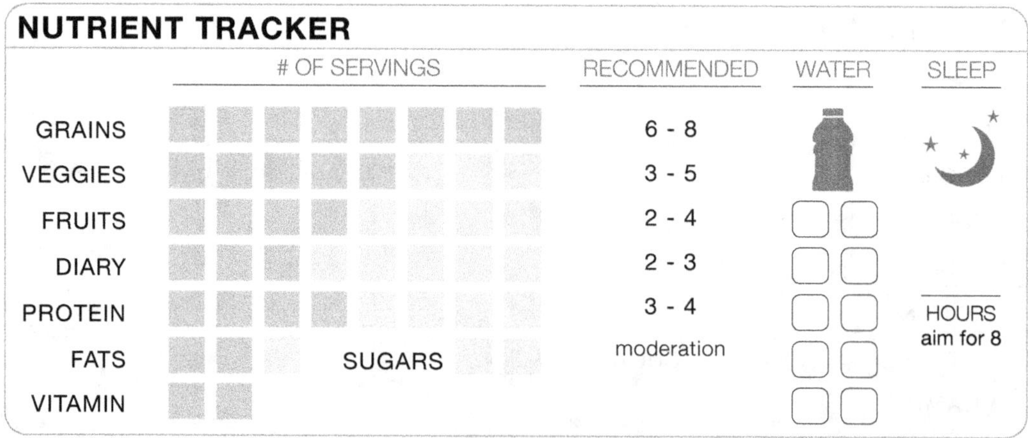

NUTRIENT TRACKER

	# OF SERVINGS	RECOMMENDED	WATER	SLEEP
GRAINS		6 - 8		
VEGGIES		3 - 5		
FRUITS		2 - 4		
DIARY		2 - 3		
PROTEIN		3 - 4		HOURS aim for 8
FATS	SUGARS	moderation		
VITAMIN				

FOOD LOG

Date: / /

M T W T F S S

| BREAKFAST | NOTES | RATING |

SNACK

LUNCH

SNACK

DINNER

SNACK

NUTRIENT TRACKER

	# OF SERVINGS	RECOMMENDED	WATER	SLEEP
GRAINS		6 - 8		
VEGGIES		3 - 5		
FRUITS		2 - 4		
DIARY		2 - 3		
PROTEIN		3 - 4		HOURS aim for 8
FATS	SUGARS	moderation		
VITAMIN				

FOOD LOG

Date: / /   M T W T F S S

BREAKFAST	NOTES	RATING
		🙂 😐 🙁
SNACK		🙂 😐 🙁
LUNCH		🙂 😐 🙁
SNACK		🙂 😐 🙁
DINNER		🙂 😐 🙁
SNACK		🙂 😐 🙁

NUTRIENT TRACKER

	# OF SERVINGS	RECOMMENDED	WATER	SLEEP
GRAINS		6 - 8		
VEGGIES		3 - 5		
FRUITS		2 - 4		
DIARY		2 - 3		
PROTEIN		3 - 4		
FATS	SUGARS	moderation		HOURS aim for 8
VITAMIN				

FOOD LOG

Date: / /

M T W T F S S

| BREAKFAST | NOTES | RATING |

SNACK

LUNCH

SNACK

DINNER

SNACK

NUTRIENT TRACKER

	# OF SERVINGS	RECOMMENDED	WATER	SLEEP
GRAINS		6 - 8		
VEGGIES		3 - 5		
FRUITS		2 - 4		
DIARY		2 - 3		
PROTEIN		3 - 4		
FATS	SUGARS	moderation		
VITAMIN				

HOURS
aim for 8

FOOD LOG

Date: / /   M T W T F S S

| BREAKFAST | NOTES | RATING |

SNACK

LUNCH

SNACK

DINNER

SNACK

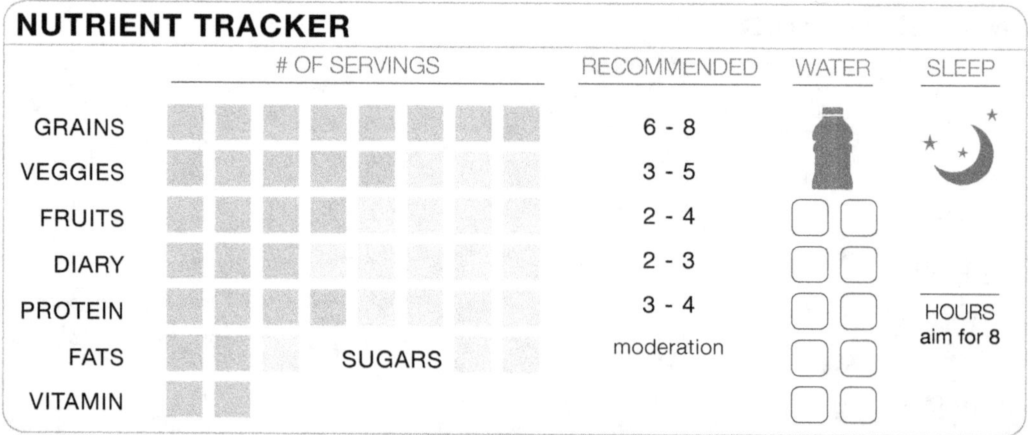

NUTRIENT TRACKER

	# OF SERVINGS	RECOMMENDED	WATER	SLEEP
GRAINS		6 - 8		
VEGGIES		3 - 5		
FRUITS		2 - 4		
DIARY		2 - 3		
PROTEIN		3 - 4		
FATS	SUGARS	moderation		HOURS aim for 8
VITAMIN				

FOOD LOG

Date: / /

M T W T F S S

| BREAKFAST | NOTES | RATING |

SNACK

LUNCH

SNACK

DINNER

SNACK

NUTRIENT TRACKER

	# OF SERVINGS	RECOMMENDED	WATER	SLEEP
GRAINS		6 - 8		
VEGGIES		3 - 5		
FRUITS		2 - 4		
DIARY		2 - 3		
PROTEIN		3 - 4		
FATS	SUGARS	moderation		HOURS
VITAMIN				aim for 8

FOOD LOG

Date: / /

M T W T F S S

| BREAKFAST | NOTES | RATING |

SNACK

LUNCH

SNACK

DINNER

SNACK

NUTRIENT TRACKER

	# OF SERVINGS	RECOMMENDED	WATER	SLEEP
GRAINS		6 - 8		
VEGGIES		3 - 5		
FRUITS		2 - 4		
DIARY		2 - 3		
PROTEIN		3 - 4		
FATS	SUGARS	moderation		HOURS aim for 8
VITAMIN				

FOOD LOG

Date: / /

M T W T F S S

BREAKFAST	NOTES	RATING
SNACK		
LUNCH		
SNACK		
DINNER		
SNACK		

NUTRIENT TRACKER

	# OF SERVINGS	RECOMMENDED	WATER	SLEEP
GRAINS		6 - 8		
VEGGIES		3 - 5		
FRUITS		2 - 4		
DIARY		2 - 3		
PROTEIN		3 - 4		
FATS	SUGARS	moderation		HOURS aim for 8
VITAMIN				

FOOD LOG

Date: ___ / ___ / ___   M T W T F S S

| | BREAKFAST | NOTES | RATING |

BREAKFAST

SNACK

LUNCH

SNACK

DINNER

SNACK

NUTRIENT TRACKER

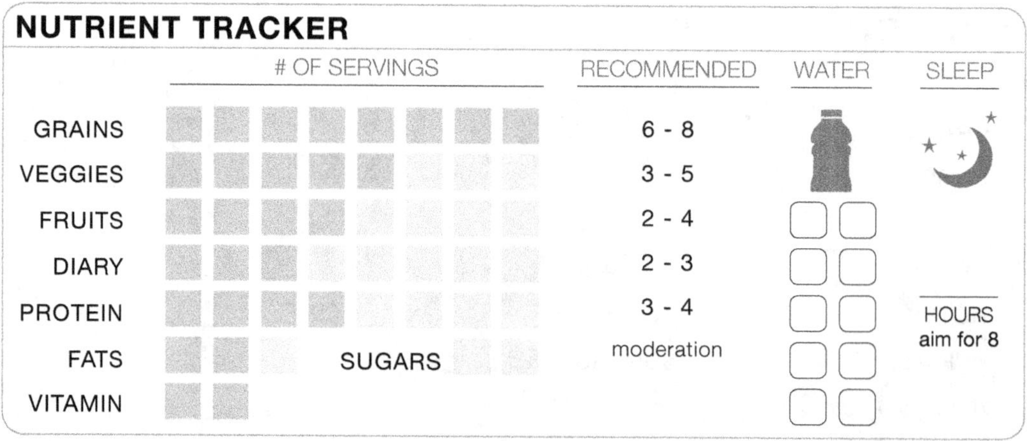

	# OF SERVINGS	RECOMMENDED	WATER	SLEEP
GRAINS		6 - 8		
VEGGIES		3 - 5		
FRUITS		2 - 4		
DIARY		2 - 3		
PROTEIN		3 - 4		
FATS	SUGARS	moderation		HOURS aim for 8
VITAMIN				

FOOD LOG

Date: __ / __ / __

M T W T F S S

BREAKFAST	NOTES	RATING

SNACK

LUNCH

SNACK

DINNER

SNACK

NUTRIENT TRACKER

	# OF SERVINGS	RECOMMENDED	WATER	SLEEP
GRAINS		6 - 8		
VEGGIES		3 - 5		
FRUITS		2 - 4		
DIARY		2 - 3		
PROTEIN		3 - 4		
FATS	SUGARS	moderation		HOURS aim for 8
VITAMIN				

FOOD LOG

Date: / /

M T W T F S S

| BREAKFAST | NOTES | RATING |

| SNACK | | |

| LUNCH | | |

| SNACK | | |

| DINNER | | |

| SNACK | | |

NUTRIENT TRACKER

	# OF SERVINGS	RECOMMENDED	WATER	SLEEP
GRAINS		6 - 8		
VEGGIES		3 - 5		
FRUITS		2 - 4		
DIARY		2 - 3		
PROTEIN		3 - 4		
FATS	SUGARS	moderation		HOURS aim for 8
VITAMIN				

FOOD LOG

Date: / /

M T W T F S S

| BREAKFAST | NOTES | RATING |

SNACK

LUNCH

SNACK

DINNER

SNACK

NUTRIENT TRACKER

	# OF SERVINGS	RECOMMENDED	WATER	SLEEP
GRAINS		6 - 8		
VEGGIES		3 - 5		
FRUITS		2 - 4		
DIARY		2 - 3		
PROTEIN		3 - 4		
FATS	SUGARS	moderation		HOURS aim for 8
VITAMIN				

FOOD LOG

Date: /   /   M T W T F S S

BREAKFAST	NOTES	RATING
SNACK		
LUNCH		
SNACK		
DINNER		
SNACK		

NUTRIENT TRACKER

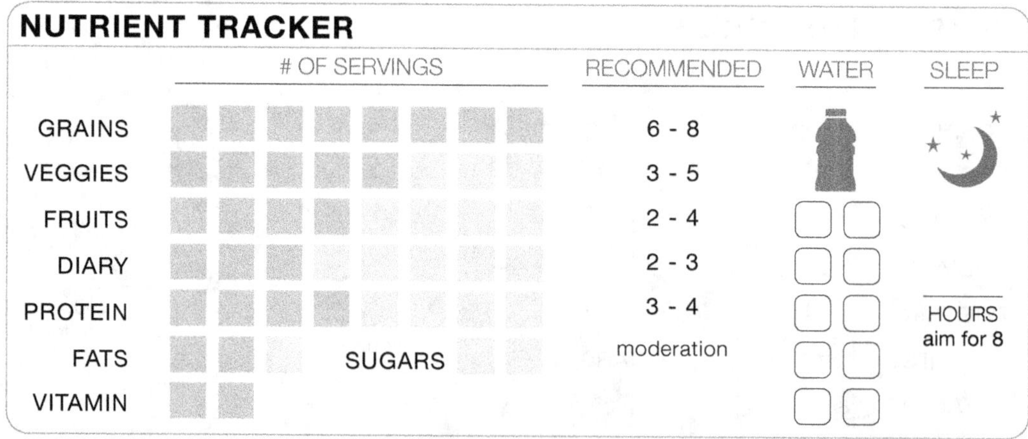

	# OF SERVINGS	RECOMMENDED	WATER	SLEEP
GRAINS		6 - 8		
VEGGIES		3 - 5		
FRUITS		2 - 4		
DIARY		2 - 3		
PROTEIN		3 - 4		
FATS	SUGARS	moderation		HOURS aim for 8
VITAMIN				

FOOD LOG

Date: / /

M T W T F S S

BREAKFAST	NOTES	RATING

SNACK	NOTES	RATING

LUNCH	NOTES	RATING

SNACK	NOTES	RATING

DINNER	NOTES	RATING

SNACK	NOTES	RATING

NUTRIENT TRACKER

	# OF SERVINGS	RECOMMENDED	WATER	SLEEP
GRAINS		6 - 8		
VEGGIES		3 - 5		
FRUITS		2 - 4		
DIARY		2 - 3		
PROTEIN		3 - 4		
FATS	SUGARS	moderation		HOURS aim for 8
VITAMIN				

FOOD LOG

Date: / /

M T W T F S S

BREAKFAST	NOTES	RATING

SNACK

LUNCH

SNACK

DINNER

SNACK

NUTRIENT TRACKER

	# OF SERVINGS	RECOMMENDED	WATER	SLEEP
GRAINS		6 - 8		
VEGGIES		3 - 5		
FRUITS		2 - 4		
DIARY		2 - 3		
PROTEIN		3 - 4		
FATS	SUGARS	moderation		HOURS aim for 8
VITAMIN				

FOOD LOG

Date: / /

M T W T F S S

BREAKFAST	NOTES	RATING
SNACK		
LUNCH		
SNACK		
DINNER		
SNACK		

NUTRIENT TRACKER

	# OF SERVINGS	RECOMMENDED	WATER	SLEEP
GRAINS		6 - 8		
VEGGIES		3 - 5		
FRUITS		2 - 4		
DIARY		2 - 3		
PROTEIN		3 - 4		
FATS	SUGARS	moderation		HOURS aim for 8
VITAMIN				

FOOD LOG

Date: / /

M T W T F S S

| BREAKFAST | NOTES | RATING |

☺ 😐 ☹

SNACK

☺ 😐 ☹

LUNCH

☺ 😐 ☹

SNACK

☺ 😐 ☹

DINNER

☺ 😐 ☹

SNACK

☺ 😐 ☹

NUTRIENT TRACKER

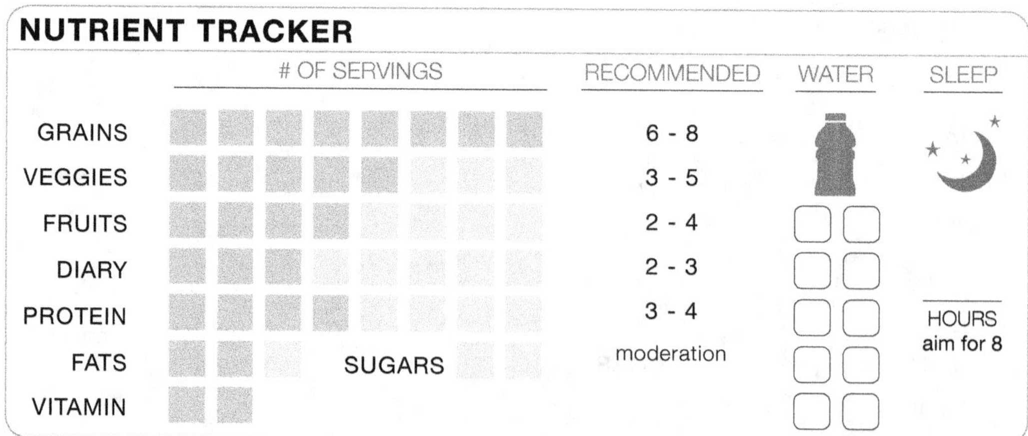

FOOD LOG

Date: / /

M T W T F S S

BREAKFAST	NOTES	RATING
		😊 😐 😟
SNACK		😊 😐 😟
LUNCH		😊 😐 😟
SNACK		😊 😐 😟
DINNER		😊 😐 😟
SNACK		😊 😐 😟

NUTRIENT TRACKER

	# OF SERVINGS	RECOMMENDED	WATER	SLEEP
GRAINS		6 - 8		
VEGGIES		3 - 5		
FRUITS		2 - 4		
DIARY		2 - 3		
PROTEIN		3 - 4		
FATS	SUGARS	moderation		HOURS aim for 8
VITAMIN				

FOOD LOG

Date: /   /

M T W T F S S

BREAKFAST	NOTES	RATING
		🙂 😐 🙁
SNACK		🙂 😐 🙁
LUNCH		🙂 😐 🙁
SNACK		🙂 😐 🙁
DINNER		🙂 😐 🙁
SNACK		🙂 😐 🙁

NUTRIENT TRACKER

	# OF SERVINGS	RECOMMENDED	WATER	SLEEP
GRAINS		6 - 8		
VEGGIES		3 - 5		
FRUITS		2 - 4		
DIARY		2 - 3		
PROTEIN		3 - 4		
FATS	SUGARS	moderation		HOURS aim for 8
VITAMIN				

FOOD LOG

Date: / /

M T W T F S S

| BREAKFAST | NOTES | RATING |

SNACK

LUNCH

SNACK

DINNER

SNACK

NUTRIENT TRACKER

	# OF SERVINGS	RECOMMENDED	WATER	SLEEP
GRAINS		6 - 8		
VEGGIES		3 - 5		
FRUITS		2 - 4		
DIARY		2 - 3		
PROTEIN		3 - 4		HOURS
FATS	SUGARS	moderation		aim for 8
VITAMIN				

FOOD LOG

Date: / /   M T W T F S S

| BREAKFAST | NOTES | RATING |

BREAKFAST

SNACK

LUNCH

SNACK

DINNER

SNACK

NUTRIENT TRACKER

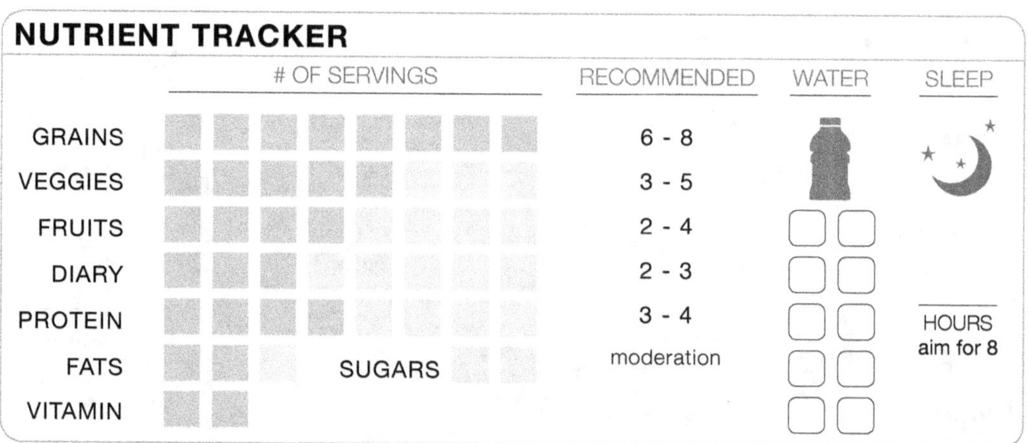

	# OF SERVINGS	RECOMMENDED	WATER	SLEEP
GRAINS		6 - 8		
VEGGIES		3 - 5		
FRUITS		2 - 4		
DIARY		2 - 3		
PROTEIN		3 - 4		
FATS	SUGARS	moderation		
VITAMIN				HOURS aim for 8

FOOD LOG

Date: /   /

M T W T F S S

BREAKFAST	NOTES	RATING
SNACK		
LUNCH		
SNACK		
DINNER		
SNACK		

NUTRIENT TRACKER

	# OF SERVINGS	RECOMMENDED	WATER	SLEEP
GRAINS		6 - 8		
VEGGIES		3 - 5		
FRUITS		2 - 4		
DIARY		2 - 3		
PROTEIN		3 - 4		
FATS	SUGARS	moderation		HOURS aim for 8
VITAMIN				

FOOD LOG

Date: / /

M T W T F S S

BREAKFAST	NOTES	RATING

SNACK

LUNCH

SNACK

DINNER

SNACK

NUTRIENT TRACKER

	# OF SERVINGS	RECOMMENDED	WATER	SLEEP
GRAINS		6 - 8		
VEGGIES		3 - 5		
FRUITS		2 - 4		
DIARY		2 - 3		
PROTEIN		3 - 4		
FATS	SUGARS	moderation		HOURS aim for 8
VITAMIN				

FOOD LOG

Date: / /

M T W T F S S

| | BREAKFAST | NOTES | RATING |

BREAKFAST

SNACK

LUNCH

SNACK

DINNER

SNACK

NUTRIENT TRACKER

	# OF SERVINGS	RECOMMENDED	WATER	SLEEP
GRAINS		6 - 8		
VEGGIES		3 - 5		
FRUITS		2 - 4		
DIARY		2 - 3		
PROTEIN		3 - 4		
FATS	SUGARS	moderation		HOURS aim for 8
VITAMIN